Catch a Winner
and the Mystery Horse

Written by
Patricia Eytcheson Taylor

Catch-A-Winner Publishing
San Antonio, Texas

©2012 Patricia Eytcheson Taylor
Published by:
Catch-A-Winner Publishing
PO Box 160125
San Antonio, TX 78280
Phone: 210-387-8189
E-mail: info@catchawinnerpublishing.com

Graphic design and illustration services by Fishead Design Studio
www.fisheadproductions.com

Published in the United States of America

ALL RIGHTS RESERVED. No part of this book may be reproduced in any form without written permission from the publisher, except for brief passages included in a review appearing in a newspaper or magazine.

ISBN 978-1-57168-030-3

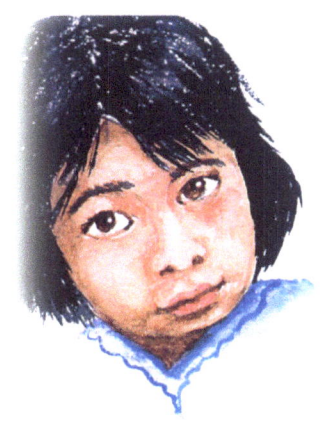

Dedicated to all children of the world

Catch a Winner
and the Mystery Horse

The Bell family arrived at Wood's Boarding Stables with a beautiful chocolate brown yearling named Catch A Winner.

Catch A Winner gave a loud nervous neigh when the horse trailer came to a halt. The stable horses and ponies neighed back.

Mr. and Mrs. Wood were happy to see the Bells arrive safely.

Jill Bell could hardly wait to get Catch A Winner out of the horse trailer. It had been a long hot trip for the yearling traveling over the hills and valleys.

"We'd better get this yearling unloaded," said Mr. Wood. "She's tired and restless from the long trip."

Jill knew that Catch A Winner needed to stretch her legs after the long ride.

Once Catch A Winner was out of the trailer, she pawed at the ground and let out a loud neigh, then stopped and looked around.

Mr. Wood led Jill and the yearling to the barn. "Here is a nice big stall waiting for her," he said.

"Thank you, Mr. Wood. Whinny, that's Catch A Winner's nickname, should be happy here."

A fresh bed of wood shavings covered the stall floor, and the smell of sweet hay greeted Whinny.

Jill petted Whinny as she spoke. "'You will be just fine here, girl. I have to go now, but I'll be back in the morning." Then Jill hugged Whinny, who responded with a soft nicker.

The next morning when the sun was barely peeking over the hills Jill arrived at the stables. She was carrying a small bucket that held a brush, a currycomb, and a hoof pick to clean out Whinny's hoofs.

All the horses and ponies greeted Jill with loud neighs. Jill just smiled at them as she hurried to Whinny's stall.

Just as Jill entered Whinny's stall, she began to laugh and laugh at Whinny. "Look at you. You're covered with wood shavings from your mane to your tail. I can tell you laid down last night and had a good night's sleep after all."

Whinny gave Jill a nudge with her nose and smelled the apple Jill brought her. Whinny finished the apple while Jill set her bucket down on the floor and began to brush Whinny.

Suddenly Whinny shook her body and the wood shavings flew all over.

"Well that helped some," said Jill, still brushing and brushing away on Whinny's body. Whinny began to play with Jill's shirt, and Jill laughed again.

It was now time to clean Whinny's hoofs that had gathered little stones and mud. Whinny looked down and watched Jill as she worked.

When Jill finished, she took a rope with a snap on one end and fastened it to Whinny's halter. Now they were ready to go outside.

Jill led Whinny down the barn's breezeway, passing the other horses, who neighed because they wanted to go outside too.

Jill suddenly stopped. "Look Whinny. This stall is empty."

As Jill turned, to leave, she thought she saw something move in the far corner. Jill and Whinny stepped a little closer to get a better look inside.

"Look!" There in the shadows stood a big gray horse. "I wonder why he looks so sad," Jill said.

"Well, we'll have to come back later, Whinny, to find out more about this mystery horse. Right now we must get you out for your morning exercises."

Jill led Whinny out of the barn and down to the pasture. She knew that Whinny had not been free to run since she left the side of her mother, Sweet Lady.

Jill wondered if Whinny remembered the last time she ran, played, and stretched those powerful legs while the wind raced through her mane.

Jill held tightly to Whinny's halter until she got to the gate and unsnapped the hook to free the anxious yearling.

"All right girl, you are free to run as much as you like. Head for the hill over there."

Whinny arched her neck and spread out her tail with a loud neigh of happiness as she took off running.

Jill came back an hour later and clapped her hands several times, hoping Whinny would hear her.

Whinny stopped grazing and took off running toward her.

Jill was very proud of her smart yearling. After rewarding Whinny with a hug, Jill fastened the snap to Whinny's halter and led her out the gate.

When Jill and Whinny returned to the stables, Jill heard voices coming from the inside of the barn. Other children had come to exercise and ride their horses and ponies too.

Jill stopped Whinny at the end of the barn while the children and their ponies passed by.

"What's your name?" Jill asked a little girl sitting on her pretty painted pony.

"My name is Penny and this is my pony, Pudgy."

"That's a cute name for your pony, "said Jill, as she petted Pudgy.

Just then Whinny's rope slipped from Jill's hand. Whinny made a beeline for the mystery horse's stall.

"Oh dear, come back here Whinny," Jill screamed. But Whinny kept going until she reached the mystery horse's stall.

Jill ran over and quickly picked up Whinny's rope. Then she peeked into the stall. She hoped someone had come to take him outside to ride. But no one had.

"Poor fellow," said Jill to Whinny. "He just stands there all alone in the dark corner. We must do something for this lonely and forgotten horse."

Suddenly, Jill smiled. "I know. Let's find Mr. Wood. Maybe he can tell us what to do."

Mr. Wood was nowhere to be found. Jill and Whinny looked in the feed room where the oats and hay were kept, then the tack room where all the saddles were. But they had no luck in either place.

Jill stopped Whinny in front of a young cowboy grooming his horse.

"Good morning,' said the young boy as he smiled at Jill. "My name is Chad, and this is my horse Skitter. Feel free to pet him. He's very friendly with other horses too."

Jill smiled back. "My name is Jill and this is my yearling Catch A Winner, but I call her Whinny." The two horses sniffed noses.

"Whinny and I are looking for Mr. Wood. It's very important. Have you seen him?"

"Yes," said Chad. "Mr. Wood is over in the riding arena with the other children."

Jill and Whinny hurried over to the arena. Jill made sure she held onto Whinny's rope. She didn't want her horse wandering off again.

The arena was big enough for all the children to ride their horses or ponies. Oh, how Jill wished Whinny was two years old so she could join the other riders.

"But it won't be long now until I can ride too." Whinny soon would be the right age to begin her training in letting Jill ride her.

Jill watched as Penny on her Indian pony Pudgy tried to keep up with the rest of the ponies.

"Good morning, Jill," said Mr. Wood. He rode up on his big buckskin horse with its black mane and tail and four black legs. "How is that yearling of yours? "

"We are fine, Mr. Wood," said Jill. "Something is bothering Whinny and me, though. You know that big gray horse in the barn?"

Mr. Wood nodded.

"Well, we're worried about him. No one every pays any attention to him, and he never comes out of his stall."

"His name is Big Gray, and he has been here a long, long time. A family pays his board to keep him here, but they never come out to see or ride him anymore."

"How awful," Jill said, with a worried look on her face. "Maybe someone here at the stables could take care of Big Gray and ride him sometimes."

"Well, that's a possibility," said Mr. Wood, scratching his head. "Let me see what I can do about it."

Jill, with Whinny trailing not far behind, hurried back to see the big gray horse.

"We have good news for you, Big Gray," Jill said, beaming from ear to ear.

Big Gray, who stood in the far corner of his stall, suddenly came out of the shadows toward them. He leaned his head over the gate and touched noses with Whinny. Then Jill put her hand out for Big Gray to sniff. She wanted to show him that she was his friend, too.

"Now we are getting somewhere," said Jill. Whinny nickered in agreement.

The rest of the day, Jill led Whinny around the stable grounds and watched the children bathe and groom their ponies.

Jill felt good now that something was going to be done to help solve the mystery of the big gray horse.

As Jill and Whinny walked around the stable grounds, she noticed three beautiful ponies tied to a hitching post. They all had different markings.

One pony was brown with white spots. Many years ago, the Indians called horses with these markings Indian paint ponies.

Another pony was a buckskin, tan with a black mane and tail and four black legs.

The third pony had ink spots on his rump and the rest of his body was all one color. Whether black, brown, or red, the pattern was called a blanket and the horse was called an Appaloosa.

Jill could not make up her mind which pony was the prettiest and which one she liked best.

Jill and Whinny stopped at the bleachers to watch a young cowboy practice lassoing a Spanish goat.

Suddenly one of the cowboys rode his galloping horse into the arena. He was hollering and swinging his lariat over his head.

"Juan is practicing on the goat now for the horse show they're having here tomorrow. They will lasso young calves," said the young lady sitting next to Jill.

"A horse show here, tomorrow? Oh!" said Jill. "What do I have to do to enter it?"

"Just go to the main office and sign up today. But you'd better hurry," said the nice lady.

"Thank you Miss, Miss . . ."

"Ellie is the name, and you're welcome," she said with a smile.

Jill left the bleachers in a hurry. She headed for the office to sign up.

"Hello, Mrs. Wood," said Jill. "May I sign Whinny up for the halter class tomorrow? It would be good experience for her and me too. "

"Why, of course, Jill. I know you will do just fine. You'll have a good chance of placing in the halter class with Whinny."

Jill decided it was time to put Whinny up in her stall. The yearling needed plenty of rest for the big day tomorrow.

Jill made sure Whinny had sweet hay, a bucket of oats, and fresh water.

Just then the loudspeaker in the barn announced there was a meeting being held that evening on the stable grounds that everyone needed to attend.

Jill locked the stall door and said good night to Whinny.

All the other children hurried to put their ponies in their stalls, too.

Mr. Wood started a fire while Mrs. Wood passed out sticks for the children to use to roast marshmallows.

While they were roasting their marshmallows, Mr. Wood talked about the horse show. Excitement filled the air.

The night slipped away and the meeting came to an end. All the children hurried home for a good night's sleep.

Morning came and Jill hurried to the stables. There was so much to do to get ready for Whinny's first show.

As Jill ran through the barn, she stopped to look in on Big Gray. He was gone. Where did he go? I haven't got time to find out now, thought Jill. I must get to Whinny.

"Good morning, Whinny," Jill said, out of breath. She hugged Whinny, then out came the brush and the hoof pick. Whinny nibbled on her hay, as Jill told her that Big Gray was missing. Then it was time to go to the arena.

Whinny stopped and let out a loud neigh. Jill turned around and saw a young lady sitting quietly on Big Gray's back. The horse had found happiness with someone who loved and would care for him.

"Oh, Whinny!" Jill hugged Whinny with happiness.

It was time for the horse show to begin. The first event was the halter class. Whinny stood beside Jill as her little silver halter sparkled in the sunlight. Her horse was quiet as Jill whispered into her ear.

"This is our first show, Whinny. Please stand still. Don't move while the judge looks you over."

Whinny stood very still with her ears pointed forward, as if she understood every word Jill said.

Then the big gate opened wide, and all the yearlings marched in, one by one. Jill led Whinny quickly into the center of the arena. The halter class for yearlings was for all the horses and ponies under two years ol d.

Whinny was still and quiet beside Jill, watching and waiting as the other yearlings were being judged.

Suddenly, the judge headed straight for Jill. With a big smile on his face, he presented her with a blue ribbon for first place.

Jill held the blue ribbon and beamed with happiness at her yearling, Catch A Winner.

About The Author

Patricia Eytcheson Taylor inherited a love for horses from her Grandmother. Because of this, she has owned many horses throughout her life time.

Patricia wrote her first horse story about Arabian horses while still in high school.

This passion and love for horses was also inherited by her daughter, Jill. Both women have treated horses with love and respect. Winning the highest award in all events in the 4-H Club. A horse becomes your partner forever.

Other Books by Patricia Eytcheson Taylor:

- *Scamper with the Peanut Butter Feet*

- *Hide and Seek with Scamper*

- *Scamper's Hide-Away*

- *Catch a Winner*

- *Catch a Winner Leaves the Ranch*

- *Catch a Winner and the Mystery Horse*

- *Let's Ride a Texas Horse*

- *On the Wings of the Wind: A Journey to Faith*

For more information contact:

Catch-A-Winner Publishing
PO Box 160125
San Antonio, TX 78280
Phone: 210-387-8189
E-mail: info@catchawinnerpublishing.com

www.ingramcontent.com/pod-product-compliance
Lightning Source LLC
Chambersburg PA
CBHW060757090426
42736CB00002B/63